THE RELEASE OF THE SPIRIT

THE RELEASE OF THE SPIRIT

REV. LYLE R. GODDARD, JR.

J Merrill Publishing, Inc., Columbus 43207
www.JMerrillPublishingInc.com

Copyright © 2020 J Merrill Publishing, Inc.
All rights reserved. No part of this publication may be reproduced, distributed, or transmitted in any form or by any means, including photocopying, recording, or other electronic or mechanical methods, without the prior written permission of the publisher, except in the case of brief quotations embodied in critical reviews and certain other noncommercial uses permitted by copyright law. For permission requests, contact J Merrill Publishing, Inc., 434 Hillpine Drive, Columbus, OH 43207
Published 2020
Printed in the United States of America

Library of Congress Control Number:
ISBN-13: 978-1-950719-64-8 (Paperback)
ISBN-13: 978-1-950719-63-1 (eBook)

Title: The Release of the Spirit
Author: Lyle R. Goddard, Jr.

CONTENTS

Many Thanks	vii
1. The Release of the Spirit	1
2. Speaking Good Things	15
3. The Soul Must Be Destroyed	19
4. I Put My Spirit Within You	27
5. Delight in the Law of God	39
6. The Weakness of the Flesh	47
7. Nature Has Its Way of Breaking	53
8. The Alabaster Box	57
9. The Timing of Our Brokenness	59
10. Expect to See Wounds	69
11. Being Broken and Not Just Taught	75
12. The Things in Hand	83
13. The Strength of the Outward Man	87
About the Author	95

Many Thanks

I want to express my thankfulness to God the Father for using me to write this book for the Body of Christ as a whole.

I also give my mother much gratitude for the insight and teaching and training in the ministry. I sought many times for someone to take me under their wing and show me the way. God led me back to the greatest mentor, trainer in the ministry that I could ever had.

My mother was a walking prophet of the Lord, and she spent years in the ministry and has spent countless hours kneeling in prayer to the Father. She prayed for me, and God used me. I owe it all to her prayers and the work of the Holy Spirit. I could not have gotten this far without the Holy Spirit in my life.

I thank my Father for sticking by my side when it

MANY THANKS

seemed as if everything had fallen around me. He too prayed, and God heard his cry.

I thank my wife for sticking by my side and enduring my pain and shortcomings. It has been easy, and yet it has been so humbling in the kneeling process. My mother built the template, and God gave the increase.

I could thank so many for their prayers, and yet I would still probably leave someone out. I thank you all, and I pray many blessings on you and your lives in reading and applying this to your lives.

May the blessings of Abraham, Isaac, and Jacob fall upon you as they have for me.

The Release of the Spirit

> "And the very God of peace sanctify you wholly; and I pray God your whole spirit and soul and body be preserved blameless unto the coming of our Lord Jesus Christ."
>
> — 1TH 5:23

When God created man in the beginning, He created him, spirit, soul, and body. As I have mentioned, the body being the home of the Holy Spirit. We are going to go into a deeper knowledge as to the three-fold nature of man. This is what we are made of. According to the scripture above, we see three parts to man, as stated by the Apostle Paul. He said, "... that your whole spirit, soul, and body..." Through many teachings and much direction of the Holy Spirit, I have been told that we are a spirit, and we have a soul, and we live in a body. Some of you may have heard this, and some of you may not. Do not let this confuse you. I am going to get it all out so you may understand what I am speaking about. So, I will refer to the three in this manner; "The Tri-Unity of Man" or "The Triune Being" of man.

A man cannot know God unless he knows "his soul, his breath, or his spirit, and his body." So, to divide the man up and to seek out the principle's areas of man, we must dissect them one by one. Let's work from the inside out. God intended for the spirit of man to be His dwelling place. This is a great starting point.

"Howbeit the most high dwelleth not in temples made with hands; as saith the prophet,"

— ACT 7:48

So, this scripture here tells us that God is not so far away in the skies past many light-years sitting on His throne, and it takes months for Him to come to you or even answer you. We do not need a spaceship to get to Him. We just need three things: a pair of knees, a mouth, and a willing heart. The Scripture says

THE RELEASE OF THE SPIRIT

that God does not dwell in temples made with hands. This means that we cannot build a place for Him, for we are not in the Old Testament, and He does not abide in the holy of holies behind a curtain. The Old Testament made many references to the "Tabernacle." I won't spend a lot of time on this subject, but the Tabernacle was the place of repentance and the presence of God. There was a certain way that the priest had to dress to come into the holy of holies, and there was a certain manner as to how he made his entrance into the holy of holies. The Tabernacle was built in reference to the Cross. If we could take an aerial view of the Tabernacle, we would see that it was fashioned in the form of a Cross in the placement of every piece, such as the Brazen Altar, The Laver, The Altar of Incense, The Table of Shewbread, The Golden Candlestick And the Mercy Seat.

This is how the pieces were placed in the Tabernacle. As I mentioned before, I will not go into every piece's purpose because it is another teaching of the "Tabernacle." The Tabernacle is much like man. And Mans Triune Being. There is the "Outer Court," "Inner Court," and the "Most Holy Place."

Outer Court ———————————— Man's Body
Inner Court —————————————— Man's Soul
The Holy Place ———————— Man's Inner Most Man
(Holy of Holies) .... (Spirit of Man)

To see a picture of this is this:

REV. LYLE R. GODDARD, JR.

God placed His area right in the middle of man. The very heart of man is His spirit, and this is the seat of God in man. In one sense, we could call this the "Throne Room of God," "Holy of Holies."

> "The spirit of man is the candle of the LORD, searching all the inward parts of the belly."
>
> — PRO 20:27

The spirit of a man has a self-consciousness "For what man knoweth the things of a man, save the spirit of man which is in him? even so the things of God knoweth no man, but the Spirit of God." (1Co_2:11); it searches into the dispositions and affections of the soul, praises what is good, condemns what is otherwise, and judges of the thoughts and intents of the heart. This is the office, this the power, of conscience, which we are therefore concerned to get rightly informed and to keep void of offence." The spirit of man is the only part of man that can know God, and therefore the rest of man must be subject to its principles. Paul stated that "But I keep under my body and bring it into subjection: lest that by any means, when I have preached to others, I myself should be a castaway." (1Co 9:27) he was stating that He brings his body into subjection to the spirit that He would no longer be a slave to the lust of the flesh.

When it comes to worship, there is only one way to truly worship the Father, and that is in spirit and in truth. We must learn to worship Him with our spirit and not our soul or our flesh but go into the holy of holies, the innermost man, and worship Him from there. That is where He truly hears man. Our flesh cannot, nor can our soul worship God without a spirit of praise and worship that comes from this place. It would be an outward show of the flesh if our Inner man were not involved. Man communicates with God by his spirit.

"But the hour cometh, and now is, when the true worshipers shall worship the Father in spirit and in truth: for the Father seeketh such to worship Him, God is a Spirit: and they that worship Him must worship Him in spirit and in truth."

— JOHN 4:23-24

This passage of scripture mentions "spirit and truth" and how we connect or communicate with God. This is probably a maze to some, but it is quite simple to understand. When we come before the Father to give Him adoration and praise, it must come from the INNER MAN. This way of worship is also called "ENTERING IN" – a term is used in the older times of ministry. When one worships the Lord, we forget about everything going on in our lives and focus on connecting with the Father. I remember when the Lord gave me a word for myself, and it was the question of "Why do we close our eyes when we pray?" The answer is very simple. He stated this, "so that we are not distracted, and we can rid the mind of all distractions and business of the day and focus on Him." It may seem kind of selfish as to what He is saying, but He wants our FULL ATTENTION. Our full attention to hear Him and know that it is Him speaking to us. This is the reason that Jesus went to the cross so that we could have a relationship and a time of truthful worship with the Father.

"God that made the world and all things therein, seeing that He is Lord of heaven and earth, dwelleth not in temples made with hands; Neither is worshiped with men's hands, as though He needed anything, seeing He giveth to all life, and breadth, and all things."

— ACTS 17:24-25

"He now declares the attributes of that unknown God: (1) The God that made the world; (2) Lord of heaven and earth; (3) dwelleth not in temples; (4) not worshiped by human hands; (5) giveth life to all that lives; (6) made of one blood all nations; (7) appointed that men should seek the Lord; (8) we are his offspring; (9) hence, the Godhead is not like any idol made by human hands. It dishonors so glorious a being to liken him to man's device."

1. He created everything by the spoken word and the work of His hands. And we can see this in the beginning of the book of Genesis.

2. Not only does the book of Genesis speak of how He created everything in existence and the creation process, but it also shows the authority and the Lordship over heaven and earth.

3. He does not dwell in temples, for He is now in us. By renting the veil when Christ was on the cross, His Son was bringing back the very thing that was lost, and that was the "relationship" that He had with man from the beginning. The renting of the veil was tearing down the barrier that separated man from God.

4. We cannot worship by the amount of work that we can do for Him nor the amount of "stuff" that we can give Him. We cannot buy a relationship, nor can we purchase His power. The seven sons of Sceva went about casting out demons by the exorcism. Then a demon spoke and said to one of them, "Jesus I know, and Paul I know, but who are you?" (Acts 19:11-22) There is no other power that can cast out a demon other than the name of Jesus. One must have Jesus inside him to exercise this practice. When we encounter a spirit that is not of God, we must recognize this, and the only way to recognize this is to

have the "INDWELLING" of the Holy Spirit. Many are scared or think that speaking in tongues is of the devil, and we can talk about this teaching later in another lesson.

5. He is the "Life-Giver." He is the one who has blown the breath of life in man, and that breath of life is the very life air that keeps Him standing upright. In the spiritual sense of the revelation, He has also blown the Holy Spirit's very wind into man. We can read of this account in the book of Genesis as He breathed the breath of life into Adam, and he became a living soul.

6. By the shedding of one man's blood and the acceptance of that blood by one nation, it is the unity of the nations that bring us into the brethren. To be identified as a part of the "family of God," we need to accept the cleansing power of the blood of Christ, who shed blood for many that we all might be saved, and it connects us all together to make up the body of Christ.

Paul proclaimed that we are all descended from Adam through Noah and that there is one God who created us all, and we are all obligated to. Since God created us all, we should seek the Lord... though He is not far from each one of us.

7. When we are born, we have parents, and if we are lost at any time, we start seeking for our parents. Another example of this is that when one is adopted from their biological parents, they grow up and begin to seek to identify those parents and attempt to make

THE RELEASE OF THE SPIRIT

a relationship. The bible speaks of a scripture that states, "Seek the Lord while He may be found" To seek someone is to look earnestly without giving up, for He or the object must be in the room somewhere. When we have lost our keys and cannot drive our automobiles without them, we seek for those keys. This is the same way with the Lord, we know that He is in the room and we feel His presence, but we must seek to touch Him earnestly with all our hearts (inner man).

8. As to the word "offspring," it is noted that we are "A child or children; a descendant or descendants, however remote from the stock." Paul proclaimed our responsibility to God because we are His offspring. Since we are His offspring, we are responsible for having the right ideas about God, and therefore must reject the wrong idea that gold or silver or stone could represent God.

9. One of the Ten Commandments is, "Thou shalt have no other God's before me." God is a jealous God, and He shares His glory with no man. He also requires to be the only god in one's life. To think that we could serve a dumb idol and expect that man-made idol to supply our need is nothing but all silly as to the amount and manner of worship that we would give it. To choose such a thing over the living God is but of one man's ignorance. Paul stated that the Athenians were serving a god they did not even know or recognize. "For as I passed, and beheld your devotions, I found an inscription, TO THE UNKNOWN GOD,

whom therefore ye ignorantly worship, him declare I unto you." (Acts 17: 23) In bringing an understanding of who God is to these people, Paul started with: God is the Creator, and we are His creatures. "This view of the world is very different from either the Epicurean emphasis on a chance combination of atoms or the virtual pantheism of the Stoics." (Stott)

Paul recognized that these philosophers had to change their ideas about God. They had to move from their personal opinions to an understanding of who God is according to what He tells us about Himself in the Bible.

> "Now therefore ye are no more strangers and foreigners, but fellow citizens with the saints, and of the household of God; And are built upon the foundation of the Apostles and prophets, Jesus Christ himself being the chief cornerstone; In whom all the building fitly framed together growth unto (very important word) an holy temple in the Lord. In whom ye also are builded together for an HABITATION OF GOD THROUGH THE SPIRIT."
>
> — EPHESIANS 2:19-22

There are just a few keywords in this passage of scripture, and one of them is.

FELLOW CITIZENS: The native of a city, or an inhabitant who enjoys the freedom and privileges of the city in which he resides; the freeman of a city, as distinguished from a foreigner, or one not entitled to its franchises.

2. A townsman; a man of trade; not a gentleman.

3. An inhabitant; a dweller in any city, town or place.

4. In general sense, a native or permanent resident in a city or country; as the citizens of London or Philadelphia; the citizens of the United States.

So, this would bring us to a word that would make us, and that word is:

CITIZENSHIP: The state of being vested with the rights and privileges of a citizen.

So, in other words, we belong, and we have rights in the Kingdom of God, and one of those rights is that we have the right to worship God and build a relationship with Him. And we only have this right by the shed blood of Christ. We cannot have these rights without Jesus.

Another Key word is:

UNTO: it is an arrow pointing to a door. However, this word is obsolete in many cases. To use the word properly is to use the word as a guide to something else. "the power of God is UNTO salvation" therefore, this is the signpost or the arrow of direction that points the way to salvation.

> "No man hath seen God at any time. If we love one another, God dwelleth in us, and His love is perfected in us. Hereby know we that we dwell in Him and He in us, because He hath given us of His Spirit."
>
> — 1 JOHN 4:12-13

What a powerful scripture that this is. It is full of power. Of course, no man has seen God at any time. Moses saw God's back parts as God passed before Him while God hid Moses in the cleft of the Rock. God passed by, and Moses got to catch a glimpse of His back parts. What a wonderful day that must have been for Moses. If we could only see His back parts or His garment that He wears, it would be wonderful. But to see God's face is unheard of. I remember two times that I saw Jesus in my life thus far, and the first time I saw Him, He was in a hole in the clouds, and he was very far away. I saw Him standing there in those clouds holding His hands up as I cried for the appearance of the Son of God. The distance was too far away to see His face, but seeing Him was astounding and humbling. The other time that I saw Him was in a vision. I saw his face and part of His right arm, and part of the Cross. I saw the blood that was running down His face, the swollen disfigurement of His face, the sweat of His skin, and the right arm

THE RELEASE OF THE SPIRIT

that was stretched out sticking to the wooden cross. I saw the crown of thorns that were blood-soaked and driven into His head. And He spoke to me these words, "you must become this dead." I have never forgotten those words and to become that dead is to let Him shine through me. We must earnestly strive to grow closer to Him. We must decrease that He may increase.

Christ may dwell in us if we open the door. And that doorway is only opened by the confession of Him as Lord "Whosoever shall CONFESS THAT JESUS IS THE SON OF GOD, God DWELLETH in him, and he IN god.; And we have known and believed the love that God hath to us. God is love; and he that dwelleth in love dwelleth in God and God in him."

— 1 JOHN 14: 15-16

So, we can see by the Word of God, that God's divine plan was to dwell in man by His spirit. God yearns for this to be so much. He desires to have a relationship, and for us to recognize that He is in us, and we are in Him.

When the Holy Spirit comes INTO our spirit to make UNION with our spirit, He inter-mingles with our spirit. The GREAT AND THE LESSER become inter-linked. Much like a big single chain link and a smaller single chain-link inter-linked together. You might be saying, "how can a small link be interlinked to a bigger link because of the size difference?" We have to get our minds out of the way and see what the true revelation is. Just as Nicodemus had to get his mind out of the way to understand the NEW BIRTH. When God's wonderful spirit inter-links with man's spirit, and the soul is brought under subjection to the spirit, they use the body as a means of EXPRESSION.

The word Express has a significant meaning. It shows what is inside man. To express, one expresses; anger, sadness, happiness, or any other mood that the individual may be feeling at that time. And this is what is inside of that individual. When the spirit of God is in us, we then Express HIM. For He is inside us, and He will be expressed in YOU and FROM YOU. The Word of God declares that Jesus is the very EXPRESS IMAGE OF THE FATHER. We are to be the EXPRESS IMAGE OF JESUS CHRIST. How are we to do this? How are we to bring Him who lives on the inside to the outside? Very simple, "Verily, Verily, I say unto you, He that believeth on me, THE WORKS THAT I DO SHALL HE DO ALSO; AND GREATER WORKS THAN THESE SHALL HE DO; because I go unto my Father." (John 14:12) Do the works of Christ by what we see Him do in the Word of God and do greater works as directed by Him who lives on the inside.

Speaking Good Things

"O, ye generation of vipers, how can ye, being evil speak good things? For out of the abundance of the heart the mouth speaketh. A good man out of the good treasures of the heart bringeth forth good things: and an evil man out of the evil treasure bringeth forth evil things."

— MATTHEW 12:34-35

Many times, we say that we speak something to or at someone, and then we put our hand over our mouth as if we did not mean to speak that utterance. If the utterance is of something good or something bad, it still came from the heart. I will not get into the power of words; you can read about that in the Prophetic Operation study. The bible also speaks about shutting up the bowels of compassion. How can we say that we love someone if we shut up our bowels of compassion? Love does not have any dwelling place within us. Bowels of compassion come from the inside, for that is the settling place of bowels. My Grandmother used to ask us, kids, if we had a bowel movement. Kind of a raw analogy, but bowels are inside the body. So, the bowels of compassion are of the heart. If we put them in gridlock and never let them out, we have no love of God, and we soon will speak that hatred for it will root in our hearts and become a treasure to us.

Whatever the body expresses is what is in the spirit and soul of man. Whatever your INNER-MAN is, is what you are. When the Spirit of God dwells within us, we take on a new nature. "Whereby are given unto us exceeding great and precious promises: that by these ye might be partakers of the divine nature, having escaped the corruption that is in the world through lust." (2Pe 1:4) The Divine Nature of God is the obtaining point of God's great and precious promises that are given to us. One of the greatest promises is that God would make His ABODE WITHIN US, within our hearts. By God dwelling in our spirits, we are partakers of HIS DIVINE NATURE, and we have escaped the corruption of the world through lust.

PARTAKERS: One who has or takes a part, share or portion in common with others; a sharer; a participator.

DIVINE NATURE: The divine attributes or characteristics of God.

The Soul Must Be Destroyed

Speaking of the "SOUL NEEDING TO BE DESTROYED," I am not speaking of physical annihilation and the destruction of the body as to graveyard dead. I am speaking of the "Independent-Action" of the soul. Also known as the "outer-man."

If the soul's independent action is not destroyed, it will react according to the outermost man. The soul is more susceptible to the pride of the eye and the lust of the flesh. It has its own wants and desires. Therefore, it has a will, and it seems to be very strong at times. We see something that isn't Godly, yet we cannot remove our eyes from it or forget it. That is the will of the soul.

The outer-most man operates on its five physical senses. What it sees, hears, smells, tastes, and feels. It does not react to the spirit within. Also known as "Carnality")

REV. LYLE R. GODDARD, JR.

"For to be carnally minded is death; but to be spiritually minded is life and peace. Because the carnal mind is enmity with God: for it is not subject to the law neither indeed can be."

— ROM. 8:6-7

In recognizing that the soul has seduced, captivated, darkened, and poisoned with self-interest, we don't have to regard it as something to be despised. When God saves man, what does he save? He saves the soul. For that is what the big war or battle between God and Satan is about. The one with the most souls wins. But as to the outcome of this war, God wins!! God doesn't save the spirit, nor does He save the Flesh. The soul is what needs to be saved. What makes the soul so valuable to have such a war in an array for it? The soul is the home of life. If Satan can take the soul, he can root out life from that soul and then fill it with death and sin. Sin produces death. "For the wages of sin is death." The soul, once saved, needs to be brought into subjection to the spirit. By the word subjection, it is the meaning of authority or control. This is the very reason that we see newborn Christians still doing things they did before they got saved. Their soul has not been brought under subjection to the spirit, nor has the spirit been

THE RELEASE OF THE SPIRIT

recognized. The mature Christian must have patience with the new converts in their shortcomings.

Paul stated in the Word to the Corinthians, "I live under my body and bring it in to subjection." (1 Cor. 9:27) to translate the meaning and to carefully dissect the scripture as not to bring it out of context from its original purpose. He's saying God controls my spirit. My spirit controls my soul. My soul controls my body. The origin of control must start from the inside and work outwardly. God must be in control, and therefore the Orders of duty must come from the head office, and that is the very Spirit of God Himself. He communicates to man's spirit in which man's spirit must bring the soul into subjection according to the communication from within. Therefore the soul must bring the body into subjection according to the communication of the soul and spirit in which the spirit hears from God. The spirit, soul, and body play a very important role in man.

The soul "feels" and the spirit "knows" the soul and spirit of man make the inner part of man, with its feelings, will, knowledge, intellect, and other spiritual attributes and connections. When we say that we feel that God is doing something in our lives, we must separate that go to the part of us that knows that God is doing something in our lives. The soul cannot hear God except through the spirit. The only way the soul can think is through the five senses. So, if our feelings think they heard God, we need to examine that and figure out where that comes from. Was the order passed down from the Spirit of God, then to man's spirit, then to the soul so that we may feel it and make a notable action in our body as to the thought? No, we must walk in the spirit to know the mind of the spirit. The natural man is enmity against God. The Carnal mind. The carnal mind knows nothing but runs its OWN course and runs wild with every wind of doctrine that blows across the land.

> "But as it is written, Eye hath not seen, nor ear heard, neither have entered into the heart of man, the things which God hath prepared for them that love him. But God hath revealed them unto us by his Spirit: for the Spirit searcheth all things, yea, the deep things of God. For what man knoweth the things of a man, save the spirit of man which is in him? even so the things of God knoweth no man, but the Spirit of God. Now we have received, not the spirit of the world, but the spirit which is of God; that we might know the things that are freely given to us of God. Which things also we speak, not in the words which man's wisdom teacheth, but which the Holy Ghost teacheth; comparing spiritual things with spiritual. But the natural man receiveth not the things of the Spirit of God: for they are foolishness unto him: neither can

THE RELEASE OF THE SPIRIT

he know them, because they are spiritually discerned. But he that is spiritual judgeth all things, yet he himself is judged of no man. For who hath known the mind of the Lord, that he may instruct him? But we have the mind of Christ.

— 1CO 2:9-16

The beginning of this passage of scripture is probably one of the most misused and misquoted scriptures in the ministry and people's lives. I have heard it from the pulpit being used in every analogy application in every sermon sometimes, and it has nothing to do with what the message is about. Sometimes it is used because it sounds good.

This passage is a very good example of the spiritual and the natural. Man can only know man and man's things by the spirit of man in man. But the things of God, knoweth no man, but the SPIRIT of God. Verse 12 states, "Now we have received, not the spirit of the world, but the spirit which is of God, (for the reason of)that we might know the things that are freely given to us OF God." He has given us of His spirit for a reason, that reason is for the knowledge of what is freely given. "For who hath (has) known the mind of the Lord, that he may instruct him? BUT WE HAVE THE MIND OF CHRIST" That says a lot. When we have the mind of Christ, then we receive instruction through that mind and not of our own.

Verse 14 is regarding the natural man. "But the natural man receiveth not the things of God: for they are foolishness unto him: neither can we know them, because they are spiritually discerned." It takes a spiritual mind to know the things of God. We want to follow God, and yet we do not know where He is because we have "self" in the way. We have our ears tuned to the carnal man, and he is speaking loudly as to overpower the voice of the Lord. The bible states that there are many voices in the air, but "my sheep know my voice." In other words, to translate to a clearer knowledge is to say that there are many verbal influences in the air and in the mind, but my sheep are well acquainted and have fellowship with my voice and will not follow any other. Paul stated to the Romans, "For as many as are led by the Spirit of God, they are the sons of God." We are the sons of God. And we are led by the Father's voice and actions and promptings. I have seen people say that they are following God, and they mean well, and I have even spoken to them on this passage of scripture, but they are not prospering in anything, and they are homeless and foodless and begging. That is not my God nor your God. If we are the sons of God, then he will care for us as sons and children. He will make sure that we prosper in all that we do. The spirit of God cannot lead you if you are living according to the wants of the flesh. The desires of the flesh profiteth little.

THE RELEASE OF THE SPIRIT

Paul learned to "live" what he wrote, and therefore we must live what has been written—living by the word of God. The more we gain in the word, the more we destroy the soul. Paul said (translated to understanding), "I live under my body by restraining my appetites and I live unto the spirit, I know who I am to look unto, I have self-control as to mortify the deeds of the body by learning self-denial."

MORTIFY: I have put down the deeds of the body. To subdue or bring into subjection, as the bodily appetites by abstinence or rigorous severities.

"For if we live AFTER the flesh, (as to chase the wants and desires of the world) we shall die. But if ye THROUGH the Spirit do mortify the deeds of the body, ye shall live."

— ROMANS 8:13

TRANSLATION: For if we do the things of the world and mind the wants and desires of the fleshly appetites to entertain the mere meaning of the world to the soul, we will die by the things of the world, and spiritual satisfaction will have no gain. But if we can see that by living through the spirit as to be controlled by Him the Almighty God and that our fleshly wants and desires must die that we may have increased in life and we may live eternally through Christ, and we mind not the deeds of the soul or the body."

It is only through the Spirit that we can destroy the soul's independent actions, which is expressed by the body.

I Put My Spirit Within You

"Therefore say unto the house of Israel, Thus saith the Lord GOD; I do not this for your sakes, O house of Israel, but for mine holy name's sake, which ye have profaned among the heathen, whither ye went. And I will sanctify my great name, which was profaned among the heathen, which ye have profaned in the midst of them; and the heathen shall know that I am the LORD, saith the Lord GOD, when I shall be sanctified in you before their eyes. For I will take you from among the heathen, and gather you out of all countries, and will bring you into your own land. Then will I sprinkle clean water upon you, and ye shall be clean: from all your filthiness, and from all your idols, will I cleanse you. A new heart also will I give you, and a new

REV. LYLE R. GODDARD, JR.

spirit will I put within you: and I will take away the stony heart out of your flesh, and I will give you an heart of flesh. And I will put my spirit within you, and cause you to walk in my statutes, and ye shall keep my judgments, and do them."

— EZE 36:22-27

Not only was this a promise made to Israel, but it also a promise to us. A new disposition of mind, excellent in itself, and vastly different from what it was before; a frame of soul changed from sinful to holy, from carnal to spiritual; a heart in which the law of God is written, Jer. 31:33; a sanctified spirit, in which the almighty grace of God is victorious, and turns it from the world to God, and from all sin to all holiness; a state of mind which is the supernatural gift of God, and not wrought in any man by his own power. And I will take away the stony heart — The hard, senseless, unfeeling, inflexible heart; the heart unapt and averse to receive any divine impressions and to return any devout affections. Out of your flesh — That is, out of you. And I will give you a heart of flesh — A soft and tender heart, that has spiritual senses exercised, and is conscious to itself of spiritual pains and pleasures; a heart of quite another temper, hearkening to God's law, trembling at his threats, molded into compliance with his whole will; disposed to do, to be, or to suffer what God wills; receiving the divine impress as soft wax receives the impress of the seal. I will put my Spirit within you — My enlightening, regenerating, and sanctifying Spirit. The Holy Spirit is given to and dwells in all true believers, causing you — Sweetly and powerfully, yet without compulsion; to walk in my statutes — In all my ordinances and commandments from judgment, choice, and affection. For our spirits, when renewed by God's Spirit to a disposition conformed to his holiness, readily comply with his will in all things, concur with his designs, and become workers together with him. And ye shall keep my judgments and do them — Ye shall be willing and able to perform all acceptable obedience and to live a life of universal holiness and righteousness.

What a beautiful promise this is. We must realize how the soul must be smitten blow by blow, time after time, as to its self-strength and government. Yes, the soul has a government, and it has its own rules. But its ruler can be dethroned by the orders of the Spirit of God. In the natural, we are governed by the things of the natural. We cannot drive down the street, where the speed limit is 35 mph, and do 70 mph upon our own government. We have to obey those governing rules or so-called laws of the land. We cannot jump from a building and expect to float in midair, for the governing laws of gravitation will pull us to the earth speedily and fatally. Fall into a body of water without the proper training to swim, and the governing laws of death will take place, and you will be drowned. In the natural, we are governed by the things in the natural and of the natural man. Not by the spirit.

To define "Government" is.

GOVERNMENT: The exercise of authority over certain existing bodies, system of ruling, controlling, a governed territory, the right, function, power of governing. Overseer

---

> So, therefore, we are under the government of the spirit. The bible also speaks of being under government. "Now I say That the heir, as long as he is a child, differeth nothing from a servant, though he be lord of all; But is under tutors and governors until the time appointed of the father. Even so we, when we were children, were in bondage under the elements of the world:"
>
> — GAL 4:1-3

Here again, we have a principle of rules that we must follow, and the soul must be subject to the ruling government of the ruling by the Spirit of God. It works as a chain of command, to put it in more simple terms. The word "Tutor" is an instructor. To put the two meanings together to define that we are under two sets of the same ruling. The "tutors," those who

THE RELEASE OF THE SPIRIT

teach and instruct in righteousness, are governed by the Overseers of the soul being the Godhead.

> "Verily, verily, I say unto you, except a corn of wheat fall into the ground and die, it abideth alone: but if it die, it bringeth forth much fruit. He that loveth his life shall lose it; and he that hateth his life in this world shall keep it unto life eternal."
>
> — JOH 12:24-25

This passage of scripture is all about dying and living at the same time. Jesus was referring to the soul dying. Not as to die and be buried in the earth. But die spiritually. He makes an analogy of understanding called a parable. In this case, the parable is about a corn of wheat. As we can see by the scripture that He is only speaking of "a corn" (the singular form) fall INTO the GROUND. One piece of Corn and One FALL and ONE GROUND. When this single corn of wheat falls into the ground one time being the ground that has been properly prepared by the master gardener, there is a process that takes place. IT MUST FIRST DIE. When the corn of wheat is covered with soil, then it begins to die. The soil elements begin breaking down the hard shell that is around that Corn of wheat, and this process takes time. It must be broken down in order to gain access to the next layer of the corn of wheat. The heat from the ground and the moisture breaks the kernel. As it is constantly watered and the hard shell is broken, the kernel's heart can be more easily reached. Once the kernel's heart is reached and watered properly, the heart begins to bring a stock. The stock then breaks ground and is then visible.

Just because the stock is visible does not mean that the stock's fruit is ready to be plucked. The stock still has much growth to accomplish. Then it will soon bear fruit. I have spent much time in the cornfields and the wheat fields and seen how this process takes place. There is a lot of preparation for this day of dying to take place. Once the stock has matured by much watering, fertilization, and care, the plant then shows signs of fruit. The day that the Gardener has been anxiously awaiting. Once the fruit is shown, there can be an "estimation" of the "fruit by the bushel" that the field will produce. And we can see that the stock will produce either good fruit or bad fruit. The gardener has much work to do with the care of the stock and the fruit. He must keep the worms and the pests and the birds away from eating the fruit and destroying the outcome. Once the fruit is mature, and the stock is at the point of maturity, the fruit can be inspected. One stock can produce much fruit. Think of an ear of corn. That one ear of corn produced many kernels from one kernel. But the kernel first had to die. One stock and one ear of

THE RELEASE OF THE SPIRIT

corn can produce as many as 5 to 100 or more kernels.

To understand this teaching's nature is that the soil where the kernel was planted was the people's representation. The kernel itself was the new convert who just gave his life to the Lord. Once he has died to the things of the world and lives unto the spirit and under much watering and fertilization of the word of God by the Gardener being the Holy Spirit working through the Pastor or teacher or apostle, prophet, etc., then he will begin to show signs of a proper death and a proper birthing by the signal of fruit beginning to show on his stock. He then will produce many kernels. This is the duty of leading others to Christ.

One kernel can produce millions of acres of fruit. Jesus spoke and said, "except it die, it abideth alone." It bears no fruit until it is put in the ground, and God gives it the increase. But when it dies, to itself, dies to the natural affections of the lust of the flesh and the things of this world, it can bear much fruit. A very familiar song says in one of its verses, "let us forget about ourselves and magnify His name and worship Him" Forgetting about ourselves and living unto and for Him, laying aside the old man that Christ may abound in us and shine through us.

Jesus was also speaking of what He was about to go through by comparing the corn of wheat. If He remained alive, all the prophecies would not be fulfilled, and all of us would remain unforgiven. If he remained alive, all of those to be born would be lost. If

He remained alive and did not die, you and I would miss eternal life. For it was in His death that our sins were paid for in full. His substitutionary, sacrificial, all-sufficient death made it possible for all of us to experience life. Jesus was saying, "I must die in order that you might live." He represented the part of that had to die out. My soul must die that I (my spirit) might live. To die is gain and to live is Christ. We must die that Christ may be shone from us and in us. To see one from the outside is to see what is in the inside. We must be seen from the inside out, and that reflection must be Him. Jesus multiplied His life millions of times. Millions of times in those of us who have accepted Him as Lord and Saviour of our life. Because He was willing to die, and there is a key phrase here, I ask you this question, "Are you WILLING to Die? Are you willing to put the OLD MAN down that Christ may abound in you? Our soul must follow the Lord Jesus in death, burial, and resurrection through baptism. It is a symbol of dying out to the flesh.

Romans 6:3-13,16 speaks about dying to sin that we may be alive in God. We should walk in a "Newness of life." Meaning that our old life has been done away with, and we get to have a fresh start in Christ.

"He that loveth his life, will lose it." When we love our lives so much that we are not willing to part with it and all of its affections and lust and attachments that it may have to live, we then lose what God has for us. We even lose sight of what God has for us. We will never grasp a hold of the world and yet hang on to

THE RELEASE OF THE SPIRIT

God and enjoy both. You either love God and hate the world, or you love the world hate God. There is no fence to straddle in this life. Both are eternal, and yet there is not enough spiritual death and too much carnal living. Are we willing to put down all our desires, goals, and to let the Lord have His way? When that person finds the "newness of life," he finds new goals, new ambitions, new dreams, new hopes, new affections.

"If ye then be risen with Christ, seek those things which are above, where Christ sitteth on the right hand of God. Set your affection on things above, not on things on the earth. For ye are dead, and your life is hid with Christ in God. When Christ, who is our life, shall appear, then shall ye also appear with him in glory."

— COL 3:1-4

"In your patience possess ye your souls." (Luke 21:19) The inner man must possess the outer man. If we are to overcome any addictions that we may have in this life, we must first find the addiction's root cause. Yes, the enemy has influence and presents the addiction to you, and your SOUL IS ENTICED. Once the soul is enticed, then you are addicted. Many cannot put addictions down because they either believe that God should take it away from them or that they just CANNOT. The spirit is willing, and yet the flesh is weak. The flesh will wrap its grips around anything that might bring it a moment of satisfaction. The addiction may have its grip on an individual's soul, yet the soul has its grip on the addiction. The soul is weak and yet so powerful. It is our soul that needs salvation. God wants to salvage our souls from the shipwreck of life. He wants to rescue you from self-destruction. He wants to "fireproof your soul" from the depths of hell. He wants to send the diver (Holy Spirit) down to the sunken ship and restore it to the surface of the water, repair the holes in it, and mend the broken pieces of our soul.

The outer man (soul) must be broken. It must be mastered and renewed for the Spirit of God to work through our spirit and use us. We cry from our hearts and make many tears upon our beds and ask for Jesus to use us when the true cry needs to be from our hearts to the tune of "Jesus break us." Break our will. Whether we accept it or not, if we are going to live for God to the fullest, ALL of our souls' energies and abilities for knowing and understanding, sensing and doing, will come to an end, and we will stand on the side of bewildered, dazed, numbed, and impotent. To die is gain. To Live is Christ.

When this happens, a new divine understanding, constraint, and energy will send us forth and keep us going. It is then we can say with David in Psalms 62:5, "my soul, wait thou only upon God, for my

THE RELEASE OF THE SPIRIT

expectation is from Him." We must pray for humility. Father, keep us humble before you. For a humble spirit before God is the true sign of a soul that has been broken and useful for Christ's cause, and that cause may move Christ to shine forth as the morning sun and set as the even moon. Christ is the breaker, and he longs to mold our soul, but we must die and be willing to die the death of the Cross as Christ died for our sin that we might be saved through Him. For He alone is the reason for life and death. That we might have life. There has to be death in order to LIVE! When the soul has been constrained to yield to the spirit, then it is that "my soul doth magnify the Lord, and my spirit hath rejoiced in God my savior." (Luke 1:46-47)

The spirit hath, the soul doth. This is the unity of the soul being in subjection to the slavery of the spirit. Unity in the body produces the power of God. Unto the fullness of Joy, the soul is essential, and it must be brought through the darkness and death of one's own ability: to learn the higher and deeper things of God. There is no depth that we cannot reach in God that is unobtainable, and there is no height in God that we cannot reach in God. Our soul must call unto Him. Deep calleth unto Deep is the noise of thy waterspouts. For God is calling unto you but your soul needs breaking to hear. Let the spirit learn the higher and deeper realities that the soul can be subject to the spirit's learning. The soul must be taught to obey, and the spirit is the mater of the whip. It must be broken. Do not despise your soul for it is important, be strong in spirit, so that your soul can be won and serve God to the fullest of Joy in Him.

> "Thus, saith the LORD, stand ye in the ways, and see, and ask for the old paths, where is the good way, and walk therein, and ye shall find rest for your souls. But they said, We will not walk therein."
>
> — JER 6:16

It was and still is that our soul should find rest, but we will never walk in greener pastures, let alone lay down in them without looking. Until the soul is broken, it will be the master of disaster. But for it to be a useful servant, the potters' wheel is waiting that He may break the vessel and remold and shape it.

Delight in the Law of God

We have been studying how the Word of God divides man into two major parts. The spirit and the soul make the "inner man," while the body is the "outer man." We have been going over some areas of importance in our previous study of The Release of the Spirit that the inward man longs for God. It cries to be with God and cries for the companionship of God. "For I delight in the law of God after the inward man." (Romans 7:22). The scripture refers to taking pleasure in the law or authority of God. Our lives must delight in the law of God. For the spirit of life in Christ Jesus has made me free from the law of sin and death, but yet there is still another law that I must abide by, and that is the law of the spirit of life that can only be found in Christ Jesus. The word law is a guideline or a boundary line within a principle. We must heed to the boundary line to stay within the law or be an "outlaw." For what is the "law of the Spirit of Life that is in Christ Jesus?" We must understand this law and know its boundary lines.

Just because we can quote scripture, and it sounds beautiful does not give us access to the spirit of life that is in Christ Jesus. We must seek out to KNOW. Down inside every one of us, there is a yearning for "more." We want more from God. I experience this very longing and yearning in my very own life. I ask God, "Is this all there is to being your son? Is this all you have? Surely the Great God Jehovah has more than what I am getting or experiencing. I am not satisfied with just standing in the office of a Pastor and Pastoring a flock for the rest of my days here on this earth. I want more from God. There is a life that Christ talks about, and it is the "more abundant" life.

We never experience this "Abundant life" for the reason that many of us, as quoted by John Maxwell, "stop short of the payment line." Many men and women of God have just settled with not being able to move into a greater understanding or move of God for the simple fact that they see no more, and the yearning and longing for more is or has been diminished. God expects us to seek to grow closer and to yearn for more of Him. He delights in you, and you delight in Him. He loves you, and you love Him. We shouldn't be satisfied with our current state of position in God for it a "more abundant life" in Him. He did not state this in His word if there wasn't something to it.

What Paul wasn't saying in Romans 7:22 was that he didn't have trials. Paul has some or a lot I should say of trials and persecution. Paul had the same spiritual warfare as you and I have today. In Romans 7:6-25, he spoke of the struggle with sin. Was Paul a sinner? NO. But He still struggled with it. His life engagements in some ways are no different than ours, just a different time frame. What he was saying in this passage of scripture is that he took "delight in the law of God" after the inward man. Like King David said in his writings, "As the hart panteth after the water brooks, so panteth my soul after thee, O God." (Psalms 42:1). In verse 7, he wrote, "Deep calleth unto deep at the noise of thy waterspouts; all thy waves and thy billows are gone over me." So, what does have to do with anything? It has everything to do with seeking God and getting to know the "real you." We must seek after God as if we need a drink in the middle of a dry desert. We have been toiling in this life, and we have been enduring the hot sun and the hot sandy desert, and we need something real, we need something more than an OASIS or a mirage that isn't there. We need reality, and reality can only be found in God, and we must seek after Him as if it will be our last drink of refreshing water here on this earth. He is the life-giver. As Jesus parked himself beside a well and long came a woman, she wanted water from the well to drink, Jesus told her of a well that would never run dry. The woman really didn't understand that she was staring at "two wells" On of them had living water, and the other had water that draws her to the point of returning through the hot sand and the hot sun. She was staring at the choice of life—the difference between spirit and flesh. The flesh will take what it can get; the spirit will take what it needs and yearns for. The spirit will never be satisfied with any other thing in this life other than God and His connection. God is the life-giver of all things, and every animal that is upon this earth. One spirit, one body, and we must know that He is the only Lord of life.

When we yearn for God as in "really yearning," our deep calls unto deep at the noise of His waterspouts. Our inner man's deepness hears the noise of the mighty rushing waters of the river of life, and it smells the very opportunity for refreshing of its soul. Our soul must be refreshed, as well as our spirit. For as our soul is subject to the spirit. Our deep is our inward man, and it calls, sometimes very loudly, unto Deep, the deepness of the Father. It cries and sheds real tears of thirst and hunger for righteousness. It needs a feeding that only God can provide. All thy waves and thy billows are gone over me. The waves of sorrow; anguish of soul; of which rolling floods would be an emblem. The rushing, and heaving, and restless waters furnished the psalmist with an illustration of the deep sorrows of his soul. So, we speak of "floods of grief ... floods of tears," "oceans of sorrows," as if waves and billows swept over us. And so, we speak of being "drowned in grief;" or "in tears."

One of the prayers that Paul the Apostle of God

THE RELEASE OF THE SPIRIT

prayed for the Ephesians was that God would grant unto them according to the riches of His glory, to be strengthened with might by His Spirit in the inner man. "For this cause I bow my knees unto the Father of our Lord Jesus Christ, Of whom the whole family in heaven and earth is named, That he would grant you, according to the riches of his glory, to be strengthened with might by his Spirit in the inner man; That Christ may dwell in your hearts by faith; that ye, being rooted and grounded in love, May be able to comprehend with all saints what is the breadth, and length, and depth, and height; And to know the love of Christ, which passeth knowledge, that ye might be filled with all the fulness of God. Now unto him that is able to do exceeding abundantly above all that we ask or think, according to the power that worketh in us, Unto him be glory in the church by Christ Jesus throughout all ages, world without end. Amen." (Eph 3:14-21)

The whole of the passage is speaking of a language from within. He prays for their inner man. That it might be strengthened, and that they might gain strength in the inner man by the searching and seeking more from God. He also prayed that Christ may dwell in their hearts by faith. Many of us have Christ in us, yet we don't have the faith to believe it. He stated that Christ may dwell, have an establishment, a place to live, In our hearts. But this is all done by our FAITH. It doesn't take a whole lot, just use what you got. If we have enough faith to say and claim salvation, then we have enough faith to acknowledge His presence in us.

Having Christ in our hearts then roots us deep in Him and grounds us Deep in Him. He prayed for "comprehension along with other saints to know something about God. Comprehension is the meaning of "understanding" I "understand or the same thing is "I comprehend." He prayed for understanding to know the breadth, and length, and depth, and height, as to appoint to the reader that as his pray went before God as you seek God that there is no limit to God and that you would understand this very thing about God. There are no boundary lines of comprehension to the love of God, but to know Christ and His love is to be filled on the inside with His "fulness." To be "filled" is an abounding in the Lord. To know more and to know that His fulness is on the inside of us.

I want to bring to your attention another key, and that word is "might." As stated in Paul's prayer, he said, "to be strengthened with "might" by His Spirit." Not to say that if we are fortunate that we would gain any measure of strength but to say that we would be strengthened with "might" an abounding strength from within. That will only come from the comprehension of the knowledge of the "no Limits" of God. Being the breadth, depths, heights, lengths of God. Might is:

MIGHT: Strength; force; power; primarily and chiefly, bodily strength or physical power; as, to work or strive with all one's might.

In other words, our inner man would have spiritual muscles, and that those muscles would only come by

HIM as He dwells in our hearts by faith. God wants to give us strength by His power.

"For which cause we faint not; but though our outward man perish, yet the inward man is renewed day by day. For our light affliction, which is but for a moment, worketh for us a far more exceeding and eternal weight of glory; While we look not at the things which are seen, but at the things which are not seen: for the things which are seen are temporal; but the things which are not seen are eternal."

— 2CO 4:16-18

We want to remember that when God comes to "indwell" man, He does this by His Spirit into our inner man. Man is more conscious of his outer man than he is with his inner man, for the simple fact that we have been feeding the outer man's appetites from birth from our mothers' womb. We were born this way, and therefore it is all that we know. We need to get acquainted with our inner man. We need to "know him." We need to share in His interests, actions, hopes, and dreams that he might have for us. The inner man is the voice of one crying in the wilderness, saying, "prepare ye the way of the Lord, make His paths straight."

REV. LYLE R. GODDARD, JR.

The spirit of man differs so very much from the outer man. We have heard the old saying that some people are said to be "rotten to the core." This statement goes all the way to the inner man. If he is "rotten to the core, there is still the "core" that longs for peace, and strength, and a relationship that is more than worldly but meaningful and true. There was once a survey taken, and some were young people and some old alike. They were asked the question, "If you could be granted with any desire, what would you ask for?" One of the person's reply was for "peace." I have been asked many times to pray with people, and I would ask for the nature of their request, and it was for "peace" I pondered many times on this request, and I concluded that I could not pray for peace for anyone. I must pray for salvation that peace may enter in. We cannot pray for one to have peace, but we can speak "peace," but in this sense, we must pray for salvation that the "Prince of Peace" might enter in to take up a dwelling place within the heart of that individual. My comprehension level had then been refreshed, and I had an answer. Not many like the answer that I give, but sometimes we are given what we need other than what we want. If I need peace within, then I must seek the entering in of the one who gives peace to the chaotic soul that is raging out of control.

The Weakness of the Flesh

"Watch and pray, that ye enter not into temptation: the spirit indeed is willing, but the flesh is weak."

— MATTHEW 26:41

Some would say that our spirit is silent, and we cannot hear it, and we claim that the problem with most of our actions is for the reason of a "faulty" spirit, so to say. Our problem is not with or in the spirit. It is not the big problem. It is not our spirit that needs salvation. Our spirit cries out within us for God and His righteousness. For we hunger and thirst after righteousness. To translate the scripture from Matthew 26:41 is to say, " watch and pray, that your flesh does not entertain nor becomes a part of the temptations that may pass by in this world that it may remain sober before God the Father." The flesh is referred to in the Old Testament as the "Spirit of Amalek." When the children of Israel were in the battle with Amalek, they learned one thing in this war: they could not gain victory over the strong army that was warring against them unless Moses held up His hands to God. When His hands and arms got tired and began to fall, the war favored Amalek overpowering Israel. When Moses put His hands straight up in the air towards the heavens, Israel overpowered the enemy. This Old Testament passage is our life with the dealings of the spirit and the soul. There is a war that goes into an array when the flesh (Amalek) wants to war with the spirit (Israel). As long as we make the flesh surrender to God and do this by uplifting our hands and arms to the heavens in a symbol of surrender, we then began to overpower the flesh and bring it into subjection to the spirit. There are times when we want to let down our arms, for we are weak and tired in our inner man, and we must call upon our brothers in Christ to help us hold our arms high to the heavens that we may become victorious over the flesh. The spirit is willing, and the flesh is weak. Meaning the flesh will follow the temptations, and we lose the war, for we must call upon our brothers and sisters in Christ to help uphold our arms that we may overcome the flesh and all of its appetites.

THE RELEASE OF THE SPIRIT

I spent over two and a half years fasting and praying for the duty of dying to the flesh and that Christ may increase in me. Was it easy? No! I had many temptations to fly off the handle and let flesh make a show of itself. I had many opportunities to fall. I needed strength, and I had no one to help me hold my arms to the heavens. I had to make myself do this if I was going to overcome mountains and trials in my life. The body of Christ has become a flesh minded and guided entity. It is all for one and none for all. If one doesn't scratch our backs, then we will use a knife in theirs. We must hold one another up. We must identify ourselves with the pain that others are going through, and we must go to them and help them through their Amalek War. We cannot do this on our own. I had people praying for me that I didn't know about. My mother's prayers had come before the Lord, and the bottle that they were stored had been opened. I thank God that I had those prayers and for the times when I felt alone, and yet I was assured that I was never alone. But I never learned how to stand so tall as to when I kneeled and prayed and cried out to God.

"For all that is in the world, the lust of the flesh, and the lust of the eyes, and the pride of life, is not of the Father, but is of the world." (1 John 2:16) Verse 17 says, "and the world passeth away and the lust thereof, but he that doeth the will of the God abideth forever." We must realize that he who can work for God to the fullest is the one whose inner man has been RELEASED to lead the outer man. When the outer man is broken, then the inner man is stable. When the outer man is unbroken, he is much like an unbroken horse. As majestic as these animals are and the appearance of strength and the performance of that strength are displayed, yet they can be broken. If the horse is broken so that he still has his own will in stubbornness, he is not broken. It is an outward appearance. This mannerism is useless to the rider. Before a rider can ever get on that horse, they have laden the horse down with burdens heavy to be borne. Some who break horses will put a saddle on the animal and make it wear this saddle, and when they can rid the saddle, they settle down. Then the rider mounts sandbags tied together around the saddle's horn, and the horse then begins to go crazy to try and rid the sandbags. The horse is not accustomed to this kind of burden nor its weight. He will buck, snort, fight, fall, get up, and continue until he realizes that he cannot rid the burden. The animal then settles down, and the rider can come to the animal and comfort this animal to assure the animal of no harm. He then removes the sandbags, and as the animal is foaming, lathered up, and exhausted, the rider mounts the animal to ride and give further training. He has built up a trust in the rider and is saddle busted to ride. Comfort and trust are instilled. If the horse isn't broken properly, he will buck you off. Once the horse finds out that he can do this, he will always do this until he is shown otherwise.

God wants to break our outer man so our inner man will have a way out. When the inner man is released, everyone around us is blessed—saved and unsaved alike. When God has taken the time to put a burden upon us, and we don't like it, we will do our best to rid ourselves of this burden so that we do not have to carry it. But the burden will never be lightened until we come to the point of "surrender." Our flesh has to come to the point of "surrender" to God. When we lay there in our burden exhausted, and our will is broken, He comes and assures us and instills trust and comfort that He will not let any harm come to us and then we can be used in war and peace.

Nature Has Its Way of Breaking

"Except a corn of wheat fall into the ground and die, it abideth alone: but if it die, it bringeth forth much fruit."

— JOHN 12:24-25

Life is in the grain of wheat; there is a shell, a very hard shell that is on the outside, as long as that shell is not split open, the wheat cannot sprout or grow. "Except the grain of wheat falling into the ground die.". What is death? We can only think of death as the world sees it. One either becomes ill or dies of natural cause or just dies, we then take the body, and we dress it properly for its ascension into the earth forever. We have the proper service commenced, and eulogy has been spoken, to make the family feel more at ease. We lower the body into the ground, dirt is then returned to its place, and we move on. That is death as we know it here in this life. Jesus is speaking of a death in the inside of man that takes place and explains how this takes place.

Cracking the hard shell on the outside of the wheat is done because of temperature and the soil's humidity. Once the outer shell has been broken, the wheat can grow, much like the burial of Jesus in the Tomb. He is the inner man. The tomb is the outer man. When the stone is rolled away, then we see that the inner man could not be held. The stone is the things in our lives that we try using to hold the inner man in. The question is not about whether there is life within, but whether the hard shell can be broken. "He that loveth his life (soul) shall lose it, and he that hates his life (soul) in this world shall keep it (soul) to life eternal." The Lord shows us here that the outer shell is our own life (the soul life), while the life within is the eternal life (spirit) which he has given to us.

To allow the inner life to come forth, the outward man must be replaced. To replace the outer man is to change him. He is replaced with new goals, new triumphs, new desires, that can only come from being broken. Being broken is a state in which the soul is defied, and the rivers of living water are not dammed up, and the water can flow freely to heal, save, and resurrect. The question is not that we must ask "how to obtain life?" but rather how to allow that life to flow or come forth. It is not that the life of the Lord cannot cover the whole earth, but rather his life is imprisoned within us. We must do as the children's song states, "this little light of mine, I am going to let it shine." Isn't it funny how we teach our young children these cute little songs, yet we adults cannot grasp the full revelation in the song? The writer of the song should have written it in this manner; "this life within, I am going let it shine. I am going be broken for the light within to shine all around this world." Though it may not rhyme, the meaning is much clearer to the mind. It is not that the Lord cannot bless the church, but the Lord's life is so confined by the church and confined within us that there is no flowing blessing to His church, and we cannot expect the Word of God to be blessed by Him through us. We are the chains that prevent God from moving within us. We cry for the will of God to be done, and we even state the very words of Christ before His day came when He prayed to the Father, "nevertheless not my will, but thine be done" as to say that we are surrendering but yet we never acknowledge Him in His will nor do we let it be done. We hold Him in this box called self.

The Alabaster Box

There is only one true revelation to the Alabaster Box. This passage is found in Mark 14:3-9; "And being in Bethany in the house of Simon the leper, as he sat at meat, there came a woman having an alabaster box of ointment of spikenard very precious; and she brake the box, and poured it on his head. And there were some that had indignation within themselves, and said, Why was this waste of the ointment made? For it might have been sold for more than three hundred pence, and have been given to the poor. And they murmured against her. And Jesus said, Let her alone; why trouble ye her? she hath wrought a good work on me. For ye have the poor with you always, and whensoever ye will ye may do them good: but me ye have not always. She hath done what she could: she is come aforehand to anoint my body to the burying. Verily I say unto you,

Wheresoever this gospel shall be preached throughout the whole world, this also that she hath done shall be spoken of for a memorial of her."

Such a beautiful passage of a woman caring for the Master. Alabaster is made of carbonite lime. This type of material is very hard even to break. Its stalagmitic formations often give it streaks of colors, varying shades, which led to it being called "Onyx or Onyx Marble." For many years, sculptures have been using it to make statutes and knick-knacks to put on shelves and even make chess pieces. They make little boxes, much like the one that this woman had in her possession. This woman had intentions to do what she had done Jesus' feet, and an argument came up. The box had a very precious ointment in it, and she washed the feet of the Master. When the argument arose, Christ rebukes the woman for scolding the woman with the box. This box contained an ointment called "Spikenard." It is a rose-red fragrant ointment made from dried roots and woody stems of the spikenard plant. It was a precious ointment. This ointment is still being put into these boxes to this day.

You see, the box is the representation of the soul. The hardness of the box is the hardness of the soul. To gain access to the precious ointment within the box, it must be broken. The soul must be broken to let the precious ointment of God's fragrance come forth to anoint and cleanse and to be of use; otherwise, no one may smell its sweetness, feel its smoothness of texture, nor be anointed with its wetness that will remain.

The Timing of Our Brokenness

The Lord employs two different ways to break the independent actions of our soul.

1. Gradually
2. Suddenly

We don't always like the latter, and even the former isn't much better, but there is time for healing, and it sometimes is best considering the individual being broken. To explain these ways for some Christians, they get a real sudden, hard-braking dependency on the soul's nature. Sometimes this manner is followed by a gradual one as time progress in their spiritual walk with the Lord. This seems to be one of those things that will continue until Jesus comes. This is not a one-time thing; then, we announce that we have "ARRIVED" for one must stay broken. And this is a continual process. As many have spoken of, the story of the Potter's Wheel is a place of brokenness. This is where our will is broken, and we are shaped to hold content. But God reveals Himself to that person from faith to faith, glory to glory. Marks are made, and marks are erased. As to the allow for the marking of the Lord. Who bought you and paid the price for you?

"For therein is the righteousness of God revealed from to faith: as it is written, the just shall live by faith."

— ROMANS 1:17

The first "faith to faith" or (faith) mentioned in the verse must be understood as its true meaning. Not that it may mean much to some, but the Greek meaning is "persuasion, credence to credence, which means acceptance." Trust to trust, obedience to obedience. Therefore, I believe we can safely say that the just live by faith in the revelation of the Word of God that has been given to him by the Holy Spirit. We can live and gain from one trust of obedience to another trust of obedience. God requires obedience in the ring of trust. He will cause the waters to sway and be rolled back in our lives and make a path of dry ground for us to trust Him and show our obedience to Him by stepping out and abiding in Him and His commandments. Living by "faith in the revelation of God's Word" is never an easy task to do by any means. For where revelation is, there abides power. One cannot just walk into revelation and expect to walk in power instantly. It is never done this way, although they both exist at the same time in the same manner and the same circumstance.

"But we all, with open face beholding as in a glass the glory of the Lord, are changed into the same image from glory to glory, even by the Spirit of the Lord." (1 Corinthians 3:18) Our image must change every time we see the glory of God. But our image cannot be changed unless we hold the one true mirror and peer into it. The one true mirror is the Word of God. By looking into this mirror, we see the places in our reflection that need to be altered. I make many mentions to young ministers as they take the pulpit for the first time, I say to them that here is the place of knowledge and you will find out two things as you stand before God and deliver the Word of God. You will find out a lot about yourself, and you will learn a lot about God. The place of knowledge, wisdom, understanding, the place of true revelation of Jesus Christ. Where the power lies.

We stay in the word of God until those areas that we see ourselves in the Word of God are altered. We then learn very quickly where the one being broken gradually takes some time to learn. The one broken gradually is the one God seems to allow ongoing daily trials until he brings about a large scale breaking one day. These "large scale" breakings are much needed but are the most painful in our spiritual walk with God. If the breaking is not sudden first and then followed by the gradual, it will be the gradual, followed by the sudden. There is no escaping the brokenness process with God. To gain a closer walk with God, we first must be broken and then nurtured.

Sometimes it seems as if the Lord spends several years on us to break us before he can accomplish this work of breaking is so He can use us fully. We don't like this process most generally. We don't like it all. We are human, and we want it our way. We cannot shorten God's timing, for our timing is in His hands. But we can prolong it. We can lengthen the timing by our resistance. Many times, our lives would go much smoother if we would grasp this concept. We prolong this by not seeing His hand in every trial and test and working against Him.

So, to peer into God's word is to allow God's word to make us and speak to us. We must be people of God's word. We must hearken unto every word and live every word to the best that we can. We sometimes would ask the question, "why is it that after many years of dealing, some remain the same?" And we are speaking of dealings by God. There is an answer to this question.

1. Some individuals have a forceful will. They do not want to let go and let God. We find this happens a lot in our lives because we

are human. Man has learned to lean on himself and survive by his own will and emotions.

2. Some individuals have strong emotions. We don't want to show signs of tears, pain, healing, emotional closeness. Some people refuse to cry. I have a brother that refuses to cry in any circumstance. That's the way he taught himself and the way that he looked at "being tough." There is nothing wrong with shedding tears, for it is the very first signs of willing emotions to healing and opening the gate towards being broken before the Lord.

3. Some individuals have strong minds. When I was entering the Marine Corps, I had told myself that I was not going to allow them to "brainwash me." I had made up my mind that I was not going to be that way. I had seen men who were that way, and their lives were a wreck, yet they seemed to feel as everything revolved around some sort of war, and the truth be told, the only war they had going on was the war in their minds. As I grew older, I realized that they had a stronger mind and intention than I realized. They soon caused me some mind problems later in life. I, since then, had been healed, and I am fine. But the lesson is the same. A strong mind gets us nowhere with God.

REV. LYLE R. GODDARD, JR.

A forceful will plods for that of wanting one's own way. Strong emotions plod that of one who is too emotionally involved in "self." Strong minds plod to be that one will not listen to the Holy Spirit that speaks or deals with our spirits. We hear something, yet we know that it is "right," yet we want it done our way. And our way is the "right way." So, we think.

Since we know that the Lord can break all these, then another question is raised, "Why is it after many years, some still are unchanged?"

> "Why we look not at the things which are seen, but at the things which are not seen: for the things which are seen are temporal, but the things which are not seen are eternal."
>
> — 2 COR. 4:16-18

Many who live in darkness can only see the dark things of life. They are not seeing the hand of God through every trial. If we could see the hand of God in the trial, then we would know that He is pulling us through. Therefore, we would have no concern. But we do not always see His hand because we are not looking for it. While God is working and destroying, they do not recognize the He is destroying the trial, for we can only see the raging war and the smoke.

THE RELEASE OF THE SPIRIT

They are void of light, seeing only men opposing them and only seeing the trial.

We spend a lot of time looking at our trials instead of focusing on the Hand of God. We spend a lot of time looking at the problem when we could gain more ground by focusing on the solution, and that solution is in Him. We imagine our environment is just too difficult for us to remain in. We see our environment unable to fit the hand of God in. But all the blame is our circumstances. We cause our own circumstances. Yet we, as humans, choose to remain in darkness and despair. We are looking at the things that are seen instead of the things that are not seen, which is God's very hand. Our prayer should be:

"God give us revelation to see what is from your hand that we can kneel and say, 'Surely this is of you Lord, and since it is of you, I accept it.'"

Some people would pray in the manner as to leave a "choice of unknown":

"God, I pray that you open my eyes that I can see you move. And that if this is your will and your way, then I pray all will work according to your word, and I will accept it."

Might I add a small note in this manner of prayer? We must know the will of God before we can go to God. We cannot obtain anything from God unless we first know His will. God does not work on "if." He works on "it is."

Another great hindrance is "self-love." Wanting to

escape the pain that goes with the breaking of the outer man. More problems arise by seeking a way to escape from the working of the Cross. We tend to find so many other avenues to get closer to God than the way that is intended and the only way. Man will always try to "take the other route." Jesus stated in His word that He is the only way to the Father, and there is no other way. So, we must go through Christ, and we must first be broken at the foot of the Cross. Man must be broken in order to fellowship with God. Man cannot come to God with Self-Love expecting to receive from God. God is Love, and He wants a relationship with man. Man doesn't know what a true relationship is. We have a general idea of what we think of "how it should be," and even then, we are still lost like a needle in a haystack. We do not even know what a relationship is. A relationship with God starts at the Cross. Many go to the Cross, but they go reluctantly, still thinking of drinking the vinegar mingled with gall to ease the pain. Nothing relieves pain like the Cross and its power. The Cross is a place of humility, Humility then steers the individual to brokenness, brokenness is the road to usefulness.

Jesus didn't want to drink the cup of His pain. "O my Father, if it be possible, let this cup pass from me: nevertheless, not as I will, but as thou wilt." (Matthew 26:39) He chose the will of the Father. He could have still walked away but chose to obey to the end. He was afflicted with pains, and they offered him vinegar mingled with gall to drink that would alleviate the pain. But he refused to drink it, and he chose to drink

THE RELEASE OF THE SPIRIT

the cup of pain that it took to die in order to give life to all who choose it. We often choose another route and find out that that route is easier than the one Christ has for us. The timing of the route that he has is much easier than the timing of the route that we think will be much less painful. He said in His Word, "my yoke is easy, and my burden is light."

Expect to See Wounds

When one has been broken by the Father, that individual can expect to see wounds, but how beautiful the blossom. Thomas stated, "unless I see His scars and feel His side, I won't believe." Jesus then appeared to Thomas and said to him. See my scars, feel my side." There is much that we can learn from this. We can see our scars and feel them, even the blows that our bodies have taken, and yet the brokenness strengthened us. Christ knew what it was like to be totally broken. Not only a broken body physically and spiritually, but also broken before the Father. He wore the marks of brokenness.

In the Old Testament, Jacob, even being in his mother's womb, struggled with his brother. (Gen 25:22). Jacob was subtle, tricky, and deceitful. Yet his life was full of sorrows and grief. He was just a young man when he was forced to flee from his home because of his traits. Twenty years he was cheated by Laban, his father -in- law. The wife of his heart's love died prematurely. The son of his love, Joseph, was sold. Years later, his son Benjamin was detained in Egypt. He met one misfortune after another. This was the dealings of God to break Him. You could almost say that his whole life was stricken by God, allowing these things to happen. These allowances came because Jacob started off wrong in the beginning. But, FINALLY, after many dealings with God, the "man" Jacob was transformed. He stood before God with a clean slate, and He was broken before God. Sometimes our scars are not an overnight effect; they are signs of many years of self-will, stubbornness, and disobedience. How much easier would we be useful to God if we could just go to the Cross and accept the breaking then trying to run things our way?

Jacob was blessed, and he wore the mark of blessing. When he wrestled with the Angel of the Lord, He would not let the Angel go until the Angel marked him. So, the Angel reached down and slapped Jacob's hip, and therefore He was marked by God. Some would not want such a mark, as Jacob walked with a limp for the rest of his days. Yet He knew that he was blessed because he had the mark of blessing. He had a wound that reminded him of the blessing of God. Each one of us has much of the same nature as Jacob in us. Our only hope is that the Lord may blaze a way out. Breaking our outer man to such a degree that the inward man may come out and be seen. God knows how to break a man to the point that all will is broken, and surrender is the only way out. When some of us were kids, and we used to please the pinching game, we would pinch someone and hang on to them until they finally had to say "Uncle." The analogy is much the same. God breaks us in such a way that we say, "Uncle." The only way that we can lead men to the Lord is by being totally broken. All else is limited in its value. Yes, you may be able to preach with such an anointing that will light the church house on fire or the streets on fire. Yes, your emotions may work on others and tears well up within them. You may have a lot of knowledge of the Word of God. Some may know the Word of God like a computer, but none of these things are going to win souls unless our outer man is broken, and God can flow forth freely.

The mind governs a lot of our cleverness. We walk according to the work of the mind, and we live according to the mind. If a man is compassionate, his emotions control his actions. We have to understand that people do not get saved or healed by emotions; they receive by the individual God is working through by the individual being broken, and brokenness begins at the cross. Cleverness and emotions may appear successful, but it is stated that it "appears successful" it will not lead men to God.

REV. LYLE R. GODDARD, JR.

"It is the spirit that quickeneth, the flesh profiteth nothing, the words that I speak unto you, they are spirit and they are life."

— JOHN 6:63

We must learn a new word meaning, and that word is "quickeneth."

QUICKENETH: Made alive; revived; vivified; reinvigorated. 2. Accelerated; hastened. 3. Stimulated; incited.

So to translate the scripture, we could say it in this manner, "it is the inner man makes one alive or reinvigorates him to the acceleration point in God and the flesh gains nothing nor does it gain any more than it should receive, for the words that I speak are for your spirit man to understand and hereby grow by and you may have life within them."

"It is the spirit of man that quickens him; or which being breathed into him, he becomes a living soul; for the body, without the spirit, is dead; it is a lifeless lump: and it is the Spirit of God that quickens dead sinners, by entering into them as the spirit of life, and causing them to live: and it is spiritual eating, or eating the flesh, and drinking the blood of Christ in a spiritual sense, which quickens, refreshes, and comforts the minds of believers; it is that by, and on which they live, and by which their spiritual strength is renewed: unless, by spirit, is meant the divine nature of Christ, by which he was quickened and raised from the dead, and ascended into heaven, and was declared to be the Son of God with power."

There is a little song sung in some circles, but I haven't heard this song in many years. Since then, we have moved on into new worship, and greater smoke and lights in the gatherings, and we have forgotten the meaning of true confessions by song. This song goes like this:

> *Little by little, every day, little by little in*
>   *every way.*
> *Jesus is changing me,*
> *Since I've made this turnabout face*
> *I've been growing in His grace.*
> *Jesus is changing me.*
> *He is changing me*
> *My precious Jesus*
> *I am not the same person that I used to be*
> *Sometimes it's slow growing, but there is a*
>   *knowing*
> *That one day perfect I will be*
> *For Jesus is changing me.*

Being Broken and Not Just Taught

No one is ever is really equipped to work for God. The equipping comes from being among the saints of God in whom He sets us under. This is often a very hard place to be in the ministry or our walk with God. For those entering ministry, you must learn some very important lessons, and one of them is "OBEDIENCE." It's a big word, and yet it requires all of you. God sets us in certain areas to gain spiritual knowledge and to equip us.

"Now I say, That the heir, as long as he is a child, differeth nothing from a servant, though he be lord of all; But is under tutors and governors until the time appointed of the father."

— GAL 4:1-2

REV. LYLE R. GODDARD, JR.

This is a position of hard reality and much chastening. We don't always like this place. We don't always like the one God sets under. But we must sit back and speak to ourselves and say, "God must think something of this man, or He would not have put me under him." But we never think this thought for we feel (remember where the word "feel" comes from") that God surely has not set me under this individual, for he does not meet OUR requirements. This type of thinking is called "stinking thinking." We believe that we can think for God. We know what is best for us. Therefore, we will go and sit under the one that we feel is best for us. Out of all of this that I have stated we can see "self" in every word of it. We can look around us, churches are teaching the Word of God more fervently than the Pentecostal churches do, but this doesn't necessarily mean they are "equipped." It doesn't mean that they are equipped in any area and that they are the only ones.

The basic question that we should be asking ourselves is, "what kind of man is he?" "Can one whose inner workings are wrong, but whose teachings are right, supply the needs for the church?" The bible also states that we will know them by their fruit. But if we claim that we heard God say, "stay here in this church and learn," and we get up after a few weeks and leave because we "feel" God is changing His mind, then we are the ones in the wrong, and we need more

THE RELEASE OF THE SPIRIT

tunability to the voice of God. So, therefore, we did not hear God say anything. I have seen many come through my Church door and say the very same words as all the rest. "God told me to stay here," and after two weeks, almost every time, right on the money, they will not return and claim God changed His mind or called them somewhere else. I would then see that person or persons and their life would be a total wreck, yet God told them to leave the very place where he sat them.

I tell people that if God set you in this church, then you need to take root here and be here every time the door is open. Too many times, our "judgment of discernment" takes over, and we leave. Again, we think that we know what is best. I have been through this very grueling process myself. I often entered a church and knew I was supposed to stay, and I soon felt that nothing was happening to advance my ministry training at all, And I would leave. Soon God began to squeeze a little tighter and made the situation as to where no one would take me and train me, and therefore I laid broken before Him asking for help. He then sent me my mother to raise me in the ministry. I had to go to her and ask her to train me. I then got started in the breaking process. Just because it was my mother, things didn't get any easier, nor was there any slack in any way. She loved me like a mother should and yet trained me as a mentor should, yet still showed the love of Christ toward me. The breaking process had begun, very painful, yet very gentle.

REV. LYLE R. GODDARD, JR.

The transformation that we should want in our lives is to be the "vessel" that is "transformed for the Master's use." The bible states, "And be not conformed to this world: but be ye transformed by the renewing of your mind, that ye may prove what is that good, and acceptable, and perfect, will of God." (Romans 12:2) This verse states a lot about "brokenness." We are not to be conformed to the world's ways, but for us to be transformed by brokenness, we must be renewed in the mind for the reason to prove the good and acceptable will of God. To find the "Will of God," we must go through the transforming process of brokenness. Just knowing about brokenness does not make us broken. For experience is the tell-tale of all things. You can tell the way one prays as to whether it is "mechanical" or "heartfelt cry." When we become broken, even our prayer life changes, it is much more heartfelt and meaningful. It gives the new meaning to "our Father, who art in heaven, hallowed be thine name..." When we are a vessel, He must pour into us, and as He pours in, the old must be removed and replaced by the new.

"Study to show thyself approved unto God, a workman that needeth not be ashamed, rightly dividing the word of truth."

"But in a great house there are not only vessels of gold and of silver, but also of wood and of earth; and some to honor, and some to dishonor. If a man therefore purge himself from these, he shall be a vessel unto honor, sanctified, and meet for the Master's use,

THE RELEASE OF THE SPIRIT

and prepared unto every good work." (2 Timothy 2:15,20-21)

Verse 21 states of something is expected of us to do, "purge himself" anytime something is purged, it is the ridding of something that is un-useful. We must lay aside every weight and sin that doth so easily beset us." Brokenness is PURGING. The rest of the chapter speaks of good Christian ethics to retain through our learning. But the purging process happens at the Cross. At the cross is the place of barren knees before the Lord and gaining access to the spirit of man. But without purging, there can be no access. Many times, I have been on my knees just crying before the Lord, and yet I did not know why, but I was spiritually ridding myself of un-usefulness.

PURGING: To cleanse or purify by separating and carrying off whatever is impure, heterogeneous, foreign or superfluous; as, to purge the body by evacuation; to purge the Augean stable. It is followed by away, of, or off. We say, to purge away or to purge off filth, and to purge a liquor of its scum.

Purging is cleansing self from self.

The parable of the Tares and the wheat is another good example. Even though it is part of the Signs of the Times, we can see the relation to getting rid of what is not useful or edible. We are the wheat, and the tares can be represented as the bad things that destroy our faith field. Then there is Judas's account who knew the words of Jesus, seen Jesus work miracles and partook of all the spiritual blessings. But the man betrayed Jesus. Just because he had his time with Jesus doesn't mean that he was one of His. He didn't renew his mind in the spirit to obey.

God works in our lives, unceasingly. There are many years of suffering and trials that we go through. For example: A man who is truly called of God who stands behind the pulpit regularly did not just get out of his house one day and preach the word without experience somehow, nor does he hold his calling without being first broken before God. If he is truly called, he is truly broken and lives in brokenness. He isn't just taught to be broken. The hand of God is daily seeking to carry on His work of breaking us so He can work through us. As God withstands us, our difficulty is that we blame others for our downfalls, when in all reality, it is the Hand of God, allowing us to fall before Him. Prayers cannot ever change God's law of breaking us.

The way of spiritual work lies in God's coming out through us and in us, and He will break out of us one way or another. It is much easier for us to allow Him to break us then to go against Him. Sometimes, through the trauma that may happen in our lives, God will get us where He can flow through us if we keep hanging on.

"Neither yield ye your members as instruments of unrighteousness unto sin, but yield yourselves unto God, as those that are alive from the dead,

THE RELEASE OF THE SPIRIT

and your members as instruments of righteousness unto God."

— ROMANS 6:13

God desires His people to be instruments of righteousness. God wants to use us, and we must therefore yield to His breaking. Though it is not easy, it will bring forth gold tried in a fire. He means good for us and not bad. He is a God of love and not a God with a big hammer waiting to pounce or pound on us for every little thing. But when we do the wrong and come to the cross, we are that much more broken before Him.

The Things in Hand

We must recognize the thing in hand. The thing in hand is the thing that we concentrate on the most. When our eyes are on this thing, we cannot focus on anything else, nor can we see it. Suppose the Father asks his son to do a certain task. The son replies, "Right? I have something that I am doing right now, and as soon as I am finished, then I will do what you have asked me to do." The thing in hand, in this case, is the thing that the son is doing before the Father's orders. He has a one-track mind to settle the thing or task that He is doing on his own accord.

 I have often asked my 7-year-old daughter to do something, and she would take so long to do it. I would soon get irritated and ask her, "why are you not doing what I have asked you to do?" To look at her, I would see that she was playing games on the phone, and she was more into the game then what I have asked her to do. I soon would have to get her attention from the game in ordered to get anything done. She would give me a long sigh and reluctantly do what I have asked, and she would do it halfway. This is very similar to our lives with the Father. We recognize that we all have those "things in hand," which hinders us in our walk with God. It could be anything that preoccupies our time, and that will divert our attention from Him.

We have the things that we feel God cannot do, so we feel that we should follow our own orders first, then we will follow God's. In the military, I learned that you always follow your first set of orders that are given to you unless others wise changed by anyone in higher ranking than the one that gave you the first set of orders. In the case of the "thing in hand," we must follow God's orders first, for He is in a position of higher ranking than anyone else, including ourselves.

As long as our outer man remains unbroken, we shall most likely find our hands constantly full of things. My wife is very famous for trying to carry everything at once. We would get out of the car, and if there were groceries in the car, she would try to carry all the bags at once. Well, the thing in hand is the groceries and pretty much every bag. She was unable to unlock the door to the house to enter. So, she would have to wait for me to get there to open the door so we could get in the house to put the groceries away. The thing in hand was a hindrance to entry into the house.

Our outer man has its own religion and religious interests, appetites, and labors. So, when the Spirit of God moves in our spirit, our outer man cannot answer God's call. Thus, it is the "thing in hand," which blocks the way to spiritual usefulness. This has nothing to do with having a god before God, as an idol, it is what we concentrate on more. When we focus on God's things and put His interest first in our lives, He can bless us. He can break us to receive these blessings. As it stands, without brokenness, we cannot receive, nor can we see the blessing coming.

The Strength of the Outward Man

We are limited in our human strength. We can only lift so much weight. I watched a YouTube video on the "World's Strongest Man Competitions," and this one guy who looked like some sort of beast stepped up to deadlift to break the world record. As he prepared himself mentally and physically, He kneeled and grabbed the bar holding the weights. He squatted down and took a few deep breaths and tug the bar in the air about waist high. He held this massive amount of weight (close to 1000 lbs.). As he stood there with this weight in his grasp, something soon was visible. A malfunction took place. His nose was running with blood. He had busted a blood vessel somewhere. He fell to the floor and was weak. Paramedics came, treated him and got him to a doctor. Sometimes, our outer man's strength can cause inner damage to us, and we never see the signs until we are put under pressure.

The weight in his grasp was the thing in hand, and the inner man was suffering from the outer man's strength. Just as the strength of the outermost man is limited, so is the strength of the soul. If we carelessly spend all of our outward man's strength, then there will be no strength left to direct others. If one lavished all his strength and love upon his parents, he would have no strength left to love his brothers or sisters and others. We find that our outward man's strength is much and yet can be used up very fast.

Man's mental strength is limited to only what He knows and what God allows Him to know. We cannot minister anything that we have no experience or knowledge in. The word will fall to the ground.

"For the law of the Spirit of Life in Christ Jesus has made me free from the law of sin and death"

— ROMANS 8:2

The word "law" here means "rule, command, or influence," which "the Spirit of life" produces. That exerts a control called a law, for a law often means anything by which we are ruled or governed. The phrase "the Spirit of life" then means the Holy Spirit producing or giving life; that is, giving peace, joy,

THE RELEASE OF THE SPIRIT

activity, salvation; in opposition to the law spoken of in Rom. 7 that produced death and condemnation.

Christ sends the Spirit; his influence is a part of the Christian scheme, and his power accomplishes what the Law could not do. He has delivered me from the predominating influence and control of sin. He cannot mean that he was perfect, for the whole tenor of his reasoning is opposed to that. But the design, the tendency, and the spirit of the gospel was to produce this freedom from what the Law could not deliver, and he was now brought under the general power of this scheme. In the former state, he was under a bitter and galling bondage; Romans 7:7-11. Now, he was brought under the influence of a scheme which contemplated freedom and which produced it.

The controlling influence of sin, leading to death and condemnation; Rom_7:5-11.

"For when we were in the flesh, the motions of sins, which were by the law, did work in our members to bring forth fruit unto death. But now we are delivered from the law, that being dead wherein we were held; that we should serve in newness of spirit, and not in the oldness of the letter. What shall we say then? Is the law sin? God forbid. Nay, I had not known sin, but by the law: for I had not known lust, except the law had said, Thou shalt not covet. But sin, taking occasion by the commandment, wrought

> in me all manner of concupiscence. For without the law sin was dead. For I was alive without the law once: but when the commandment came, sin revived, and I died. And the commandment, which was ordained to life, I found to be unto death. For sin, taking occasion by the commandment, deceived me, and by it slew me."
>
> — ROM 7:5-11

But why is this law of the Spirit of Christ Jesus ineffectual in some people? Again, the strength of the outward man can overpower by his will and emotions. "That the righteousness of the law might be fulfilled in us who walk not after the flesh, but after the Spirit." (Romans 8:4) Though there is a law for a law, it can be broken. Many live to violate laws, and therefore they are outlaws. The answer to the question is laid out simply in the word of God. "they walk after the flesh not after the spirit." They walk after the appetites of the flesh.

The law of the Spirit of Life works effectively only for those who are spiritual, that is, those who mind the things of the Spirit. So, to "mind" the things of the Spirit is to say that we either obey the things of the Spirit or that we set the things of the Spirit within our minds. Those who are intent on carnal (fleshly, soulish) things can be attentive to spiritual things. Those who are intent upon spiritual things come under the force of the law of the Holy Spirit. So, if we are committed to the things of the Spirit, then the Holy Spirit will enforce the Word of God in our lives.

As long as we have the "thing in hand," we cannot do God's work for the "thing in hand," our members are unable to work. We may be going through all the motions of serving God and seemingly trying, but the blessings of God won't come. Going through the motions does not produce a good return. According to the number of "things in hand," strength for serving God either decreases or increases. So, the thing in hand becomes the hindrances and not at all a small one, and it grows bigger and bigger.

"Ye did run well: who did hinder you that ye should not obey the truth?"

— GALATIANS 5:7

The Christian life is often represented as a race. Paul means here that they began the Christian life with ardor and zeal. Who did hinder you – or who did "Drive you back?" The word used here means properly to beat or drive back. Hence, it means to hinder, check, or retard. Dr. Doddridge remarks that this is "an Olympic expression, and properly signifies 'coming across the course' while a person is running in it, in such a manner as to jostle, and throw him out of the way." Paul asks, with emphasis, who it could have been that retarded them in their Christian course, implying that it could have been done only by their own consent, or that there was really no cause why they should not have continued as they began. The true system of justification by faith in the Redeemer, that you should have turned aside and embraced the dangerous errors regarding the necessity of obeying Moses's laws.

Our hearts cry should be to the Lord, break us, God, make us, and mold us into a vessel for use.

> *Je---sus. Use me, o Lord, don't refuse me,*
> *Surely there's a work that I can do.*
> *Even tho' it's humble*
> *Lord help my will to crumble,*
> *Tho' the cost be great, I'll work for You.*
>
> *Dear Lord, I'll be a witness if You will help*
> *   my weakness.*
> *I know that I'm not worthy, Lord, of You.*
>
> *By eyes of faith I see You, on the cross of*
> *   cal-v'ry, dear*
> *Lord, I cry, "let me Your servant be"*
> *Je---sus. Use me,*
> *O Lord, don't refuse me,*
> *Surely there's a work that I can do.*
> *Even tho' it's humble*

THE RELEASE OF THE SPIRIT

Lord help my will to crumble,
Tho' the cost be great, I'll work for You."
He's the Lily of the valley

The Bright and Morning Star
He's the Fairest of ten thousand to my soul'
He's the beautiful Rose of Sharon, he's all the
    world to me,
but best of all, He is my coming King

Je---sus. use me,
O Lord, don't refuse me,
Surely there's a work that I can do.
Even tho' it's humble
Lord help my will to crumble,
Tho' the cost be great, I'll work for You."

Je---sus. Use me,
O Lord, don't refuse me,
Surely there's a work that I can do.
Even tho' it's humble
Lord help my will to crumble,
Tho' the cost be great, I'll work for You."

About the Author

Lyle R. Goddard Jr. was a young man with a vision and a dream. From his youth, he set out to learn the Word of God. Lyle was born in Aurora, Missouri. Rev. Louise Conley Eustler Pastored the Church where his parents were attending. Sister Eustler prophesied over his life when Lyle was born to preach the Gospel and a prophet's call upon his life.

Lyle ran from the Lord for many years before realizing that he had better heed to the calling. Lyle served in the United States Marine Corps during the time of Desert Storm, being a veteran of the force. Lyle was not a Christian at this time, and the call began to weigh heavily upon his heart and life. Lyle began to drive a truck when his parents lived in Oklahoma, moving from Texas to live near their two sons.

Lyle received Christ into his life, began pursuing his call, and enrolled in a correspondence course with Rhema Bible School. Here he learned a foundation for his ministry. He would take his studies everywhere he went. He would study while his truck was being loaded and unloaded. God began to work in his life, and the hunger within him began to get greater. Soon he began to search out places to preach. He pursued a Bachelor of Arts in Biblical studies by Correspondence. God would never allow Lyle to go to a school physically. God taught him through his mother and by the Holy Spirit. Lyle would preach any place where he was given the space. He suffered many hassles with trying to find a church to let him use the pulpit. Lyle then began to feel the leading of the Lord to open His own charter ministry. He had a desire to help train young ministers in the ministry. As Lyle earnestly took this to the Lord, his mother, who was also a minister and trained him, spoke to him and said that the "Warriors of the Way" name kept coming to her. Lyle went home and pondered on the name and presented it before the Lord. God gave Lyle assurance that this was the name for the ministry. On November 7th, 2001, this ministry was born.

Lyle fell away from the Lord in 2009 after his mother had passed away. He became an alcoholic, and his life went downhill at a fast rate. He moved to Nebraska and drank his life away. Lyle was hurt and very angry at God for the passing of his mother. Lyle remarried in the year 2012 to Traci DeHart. They had a beautiful daughter who they named Jaycey, who was born in 2013. They both ran a bar. Lyle also worked a full-time job and continued to take his anger out against God by continually drinking. Lyle was found sitting in front of a cemetery with a loaded pistol, with all intentions of suicide. With no one knowing his whereabouts, his wife discovered his position, and God saved him from destruction.

Soon they lost two vehicles and a mower, were living in a very cold house and were behind on everything they had. While being in a drunken state, constantly fighting the call. Lyle felt the call knocking on his heart's door much greater than he had ever felt. The call never left, and it was time for him to come home to Christ. He and his wife Traci gave their hearts to God. Lyle then began to preach in his home by holding Bible studies. The house began to fill, and the power of God began to move and retrain him and refresh him at an accelerated rate. They soon had to decide to stay or go as God directed. On June 8th of 2017, they had decided to leave Nebraska the next morning. They had a borrowed vehicle, $400 in their pockets, their clothes, a child, and a dog. They were on their way to Ada, Oklahoma.

As they moved in with Lyle's sister, sleeping on the living room floor on an air mattress, God began to move. They pursued their own home or something they could call home. There was much resistance until all resources were exhausted, and no results were found. They began to see the hand of God move in their lives. They soon moved into their own apartment, where Lyle continued to resurrect Warriors of the Way ministries. They began to have services in Lyle's sister's living room. In a short time, God moved them to a storefront building where he experienced tremendous growth and walked by faith as God provided every month. He experienced much resistance and never gave up. He trained his leaders in his ministry and trained them not to give up no matter the cost. He received threats and even been called names by the body of Christ. Even Pastors belittled him and his wife and his ministry. He never buckled under the pressure but pursued after God much greater and harder. Covid-19 came to Ada, Oklahoma. While churches were praying for their decision to shut their doors, Lyle turned up the volume and held the doors open, and continued to preach every night for 19 days until God said stop. Greater revelation and prophecy came through those days through Lyle, and it was very powerful.

People would turn their backs on Lyle, but he never gave up on God or his purpose. Souls and strengthening the body of Christ to rise against a worldwide pandemic are the purpose of his calling. After two and a half years, God provided a Church building where he assumed the position as the Senior Pastor of Highway Tabernacle Community Church. He has since the started live streams of teaching and continues the call of God on his life. Lyle is in the process of writing many books, training ministers, and teaching through live streams; calling out the word of God as he has always done with the manifested power of the Holy Spirit. Lyle's only mindset is Christ and to fulfill the call of the raising of the sons of God.

1

www.ingramcontent.com/pod-product-compliance
Lightning Source LLC
Chambersburg PA
CBHW052112110526
44592CB00013B/1574